Reasons My Cat Is Mad

Reasons My Cat Is Mad

Heloísa Nora

unbound

First published in 2020

Unbound
Level 1, Devonshire House, One Mayfair Place, London W1J 8AJ
www.unbound.com
All rights reserved

Text design by PDQ Digital Media Solutions Ltd

A CIP record for this book is available from the British Library

ISBN 978-1-80018-004-8 (hardback)
ISBN 978-1-80018-005-5 (ebook)

Printed in Great Britain by CPI Group (UK)

1 3 5 7 9 8 6 4 2

With special thanks to Jason Chan

Introduction

Poorly Drawn Cats was born on Twitter, in the form of a tiny account (@poorlycatdraw) where I would post funny drawings of cats to make my friends laugh. I started the account during my first year living apart from my parents (and my cat Pandora), and found it was a good way to feel less lonely in my new environment.

Then, one day, I made a drawing that changed everything: the 'snat', or snake cat. I woke up to find I suddenly had thousands of followers, more than I could possibly have imagined! There were 'snat' tattoos, and people asking me to draw their cats – I couldn't believe I was able to create something people would appreciate that much.

From an account I made so I wouldn't feel alone, to an account that makes me smile every single day. People have been incredibly caring and encouraging, and I'm so grateful for everything we've created together.

Each and every cat in this book was drawn by me with love – I hope you have as much fun looking at them as I did making them. The ideas came from Twitter; from mentions and replies; from Pandora and Polenta being silly cats; from walks on the street with my boyfriend and car rides with my family; and from the kind people who supported this project by commissioning drawings for the 'Reasons Your Cat Is Mad' and 'Hall of Fame' sections. This book is a way of trying to thank you for everything you've done.

This is our book; these are our poorly drawn cats.

Heloísa, April 2020

My cat is mad because: she will not be cooed at and treated like a pet when she is an apex predator, capable of destroying everyone in her path.

My cat is mad because: bath time.

My cat is mad because: I touched his beans.

My cat is mad because: I'm working on his bed.

My cat is mad because: he's not familiar
with birthdays. Or candles. Or fire.

My cat is mad because: he should've bought that boat.

My cat is mad because: I kept booping her nose.

My cat is mad because: boots.

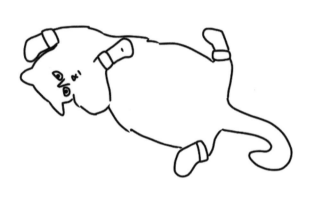

My cat is mad because: he was mistaken for a loaf of bread.

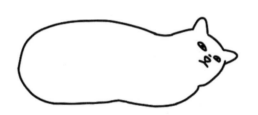

My cat is mad because: car ride.

My cat is mad because: his name is Cheese and he doesn't even like cheese.

My cat is mad because: I turned him into a dinosaur.

My cat is mad because: she wants to be in the room but can't open doors.

My cat is mad because: I'm drawing him with my eyes closed.

My cat is mad because: he hates being the blanket ghost.

My cat is mad because: I don't appreciate his gifts.

My cat is mad because: he forgot how to cat.

My cat is mad because: you don't love yourself enough.

My cat is mad because: she hasn't been fed for two million years. (More like two hours.)

My cat is mad because: the cat in
the mirror keeps copying her.

My cat is mad because: *n o b a n a n a*.

My cat is mad because: he hates the outside.

My cat is mad because: I didn't let him eat a plastic bag for lunch.

My cat is mad because: I'm watching him poop.

My cat is mad because:
I made her into a purrito.

My cat is mad because: she knows
I'm behind the laser pointer.

My cat is mad because: the revolution hasn't started yet.

My cat is mad because: *s a l a d*.

My cat is mad because: he wants
more than a little salami.

My cat is mad because: societal norms say he can't sit like a human.

My cat is mad because: you said
his smile is a little scary.

My cat is mad because: he smol.

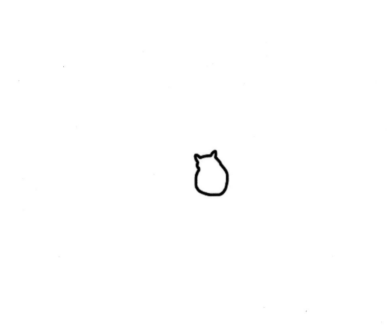

My cat is mad because: its teleportation is taking too long.

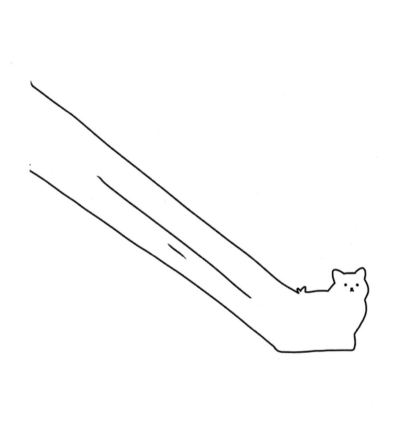

My cat is mad because: he has no thumbs and can't play video games.

My cat is mad because: we trimmed her claws and she can't wake us up in the middle of the night scratching them on the couch.

My cat is mad because: the vet had to touch his butt.

My cat is mad because: humans laugh
when he walks like them.

My cat is mad because: she wants to drink my water. From my glass.

My cat is mad because: her wet food was too wet.

My cat is mad because: I have bought her the wrong cat food. Salmon was the right food last week. Now it is chicken. Keep up.

My cat is mad because: the plate was empty.

My cat is mad because: I coughed
and disturbed her peace.

My cat is mad because: he showed me his beans and didn't get a response.

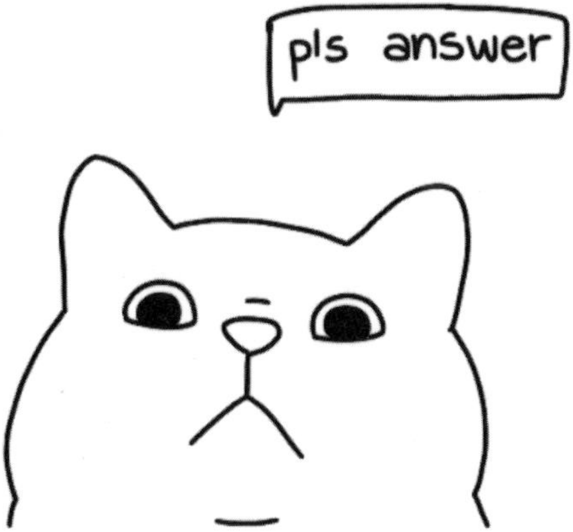
pls answer

My cat is mad because: meowdy.

My cat is mad because: it's not a phase, Mom.

My cat is mad because: you're killing his vibe.

My cat is mad because: an ancient curse decided to overtake him right before dinner time.

My cat is mad because: she doesn't like being a unicorn.

My cat is mad because: he doesn't like selfies.

My cat is mad because: well…
that's the way she is.

Reasons Your Cat Is Mad

The Butcher is mad because: his breakfast is late. Lucy is mad because: the vase of flowers is in her spot.

Carter is mad because: he isn't allowed to squirm under the back fence and explore the neighbourhood.

Mr Biggie Smalls is mad because:
someone ate all his Pringles.

Snow is mad because: gravity is against her.

Toast is mad because: you're doing it wrong. Do it right. DON'T do it wrong.

Whiskey Tango Foxtrot is mad because: we won't let her outside to roll in the dirt.

Hall of Fame

Archer

BooBoo

Calliope

Casper

Cheetarah

Clara

Cooper

Curry

Dave

Dude

Judy

Lola

Louis

Luna and Willa

Matilda

Mr Snow

Onyx

Pookie

Poppy

Princess Sadie (2020)

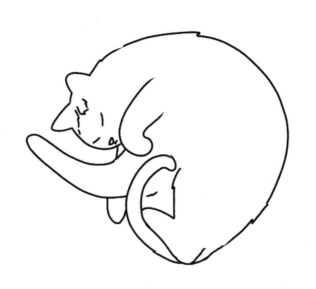

Priscilla

Rosie

Rue

Ruffles

Tippy and Tubby

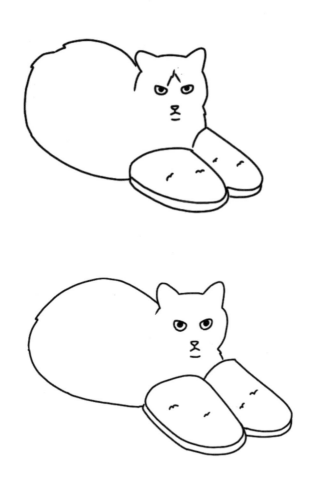

Toast

Tortilla

Willow

Acknowledgements

I wanted to add some thank yous.

Thanks to those who sent me their ideas and cat pictures on Twitter: you've helped me make this dream come true. *Reasons My Cat Is Mad* would be nothing without you.

Thanks to those who pledged for the book, and all those who have supported my artwork over the years.

Thanks to my English teachers for giving me the skills to produce a book in English.

Thanks to my mom Zuleide, my dad Danilo, my sister Gabriela, my boyfriend Lucas, and all my friends and family for believing in me.

A Note on the Author

Heloísa Nora is a law student living in Brazil. She is the illustrator behind the hugely popular Poorly Drawn Cats account on Twitter.

@poorlycatdraw

Unbound is the world's first crowdfunding publisher, established in 2011.

We believe that wonderful things can happen when you clear a path for people who share a passion. That's why we've built a platform that brings together readers and authors to crowdfund books they believe in – and give fresh ideas that don't fit the traditional mould the chance they deserve.

This book is in your hands because readers made it possible. Everyone who pledged their support is listed below. Join them by visiting unbound.com and supporting a book today.

Ben Bird Person

Ellen Berg

Piers Bergquist

Emerald Betts

Marcel Binkele

Sam Birdwell

Julie Black

Joshua Blanck

Monica Block

Bo the Meowjesty and Eve
the Princess

Anita Boeira

Lea Bohn

Leila Bond

Christen Boniface

Trina Bonman

Alana Bothun-Hill

Toni Boughton

Clara Bouillet Lortet

Sara Bovi

Camilla Boyle

Gillian Braden

Ben Brandwood

Gabrielle Brest

Elena Breuza

Addie Brewer

Otto Bricking

Jess Brooks

Lindsay Brown

Martin Brown

McLean Brown

Kelli Bryan

Sarah Bunch

Alex Burton-Keeble

Ashlynn Butler

Patrick Cairns

Ian Calcutt

Corin Caliendo

Jessica Carr

Manga, Ani, Moira, Astrid
& Nate Catt

Katie Cavanagh

Kelsey Chan

Cici Chao

Charlie

Sonya Chaudhary

Alfred Chavez

Patricia Chavez

Nicholas Cheek

Grace Chen

Ethan Christensen

Claudia, Margaret, & Anne

Emma Coley

Mackenzie Colwell

Joshua Conner

Christine Cossette

Daniel Coutinho

Robert Cox

Jane Crawford

John Crawford

Melanie Croos-Dabrera

Linda Crux

Curious Zelda

Elizabeth Curtis

John Danziger

Dashiell & Hyde

Amanda Daunais

Stephanie De Brito Leal

Michael Dean

Ben DeFever
Shane DeLeon
Liz Denholm
Kirsi DeVries
Jennifer Diagostino
Ricardo Diaz-Albertini
Sean Dobbs
Liz Doherty
Veerle Donker
Jessica Duchen
Lottie Duren
Alyce Eaton
Cara Eckenrode
Sarah Edwards
Emily Elias
Eric, Franklin, and Satsuki
Rachel Evans
Lara F
Marija Ferber
Salome Fernandez
Lizzy Finn
Ian Fitch
Matthew Flambard

Brenda Fogg
John Fowler
Oscar Fowler
Tigerlily Fowler
Nadine Frassetto
Jason Frazier
Roberta Freese
Bjarki Freki
Jasmine Friedrich
Rui Fu
Sarah Fuchs
Karin Fujii
Allison Funneman
Fiona Galloway
Scoota Galloway
Daniela Galvan
Mark Gamble
Fuzzy Gerdes
Emil Gerth
Katie Giles
John Gill
Adam Glynn
A Goldie

Holly Goodman
Andrea Gordon
Genny Gordon
Allison Gore
Virginia Goss
Nicole Grana
Jonathan Grant
Bethany Graves
Laika Ereira Green
Rose Green
Zoe Greenfield
Lisa Grimmer
Davonna Grubbs
Elizabeth Hagerty
Anoria Haick
Jessica Halleck
Claire Hammack
Eli Hanna
Kate Hannum
Julie Hardisty
Jayne Harper
Mel Harper
Becca Harper-Day

Andy Hart
Victoria Hart
Jessica Hately
Amy Hayward-Downs
Robert Hebert
Iris Herchenroeder
My Beloved Cat Hercules
Vanessa Heron
Justine Hickey
John Hoare
Michael Hokama
Ken Hollan
Samantha Holland
Shayne Holley
Michelle Hom
Aimee-marie Hopkins
Nicole Horn
Andrew Huang
Sarah Hudak
Talia Hughes
Sarah Hutchinson
Icarus
Michael Imber

Elyse Ireland
Jackrabbit
Brooke Jackson
Integress Jen
Jess & Zach
Jamie Jiang
Dewey Johns
Parsley Johns
Jamie Johnson
Abbey Joiner
Anneke Jong
Ellen Jurczak
Aspasia Karamalegos
Kasia
Katie-May & Flossie Boyd
Nate Kellum
Maureen Kendzierski
Matthew Kenlan
Ellen Kern
Mary Kersey
Dan Kieran
Dean Kiner
Jeremy Kitchen

Desi Klaer
Eddie Kohler
Alexandros Kotzias
Mark Krieger
Barbara Kriesten
Lauren Krucke
Renee Krulich
Pierre L'Allier
Nicole LaChance
Kim Ladin
Kristin Laemmert
Twinkle Lam
Samantha Lattieri
Emma LD
Ban Lee
Glen Lee
Jane Lehr
Shandelle Leigh
Fiona Lensvelt
Buster Lewis
Megan Lewis
Catherine Li
Michael Li

Li'l B the Cat

Derek Lieu

Perry Liles

Mary Lin

Rob Lion

Nicole Lipson

Sandra Little

Athena Lo

Jes LO

Christine Long

Gemma Lovegrove

Jessica Lovelace

Rachel Lundeen

Jamie Macleod

Maddie & Austin

Bethany Madigan

Angela Mai

Aaron Malone

Philippa Manasseh

Bellamy Mannis

Erica Mannis

Brenton Mantone

Lou Marcotte

Nicola Mariana

Ana Martinez

Anjelica Martinez

Paula Matthewson

Katie Matthias

Brad Matthies

Caroline Maughon

Steve Maxwell

Emily May

Leo McCabe

Brianna McCaffrey

William McCarthy

Yvonne Carol McCombie

Kimberly McDaniel

Kate McGann

Jen McKernan

Katrina McMillin

Ruarri Meatheringham

Leigh Medway

Walter Mendoza Jesus

Petet Menking

Marcia Menter

Abbie Merryman

Becca Miller

Chadwick Miller

Jade Miller

Jessica Miller

Mincarlo and Merrick

John Mitchinson

Evgeniya Molodykh

Cult Moo

Ana K. Morales

Kathryn Mordecai

Rhianna Moreland

Morgana

Meridith Morrissey

Sasha Moss

Ryan Moursund

Kristen Muenz

Jennifer & Jason Mulligan

Payton Murillo

Maureen Murphy

Kathy Nagle

Sam Nagle

Lindsey Narva

Carlo Navato

Belinda Naylor

Christopher Nelson

Luisa Neves

AngelBear Newcomb

Melanie Jane Newcomb

Bmo + Hannah
Newman-Smart

Cassandra Ng

Sinéad nic Oireachtaigh

Jen Nichols

David Nickson

Nicole, Stormy,
& Fiddler

Laura Nighan

EM NightCat

Kitty Nishimura

Jacque Nodell

Chloe Nunez

Debbe Nye

Ben O'Neill

Colin Oaten

Heather Oldfield

Lexie Oliva

Ben Oram

Kersten Ostwald

Théo Paponnet

Sara Patterson

Victoria Paul

Joy Pemberton

Chelsea K. Perez

Akia Pichon

Jenny Pierson

Helen Plumtree

Poirot and Captain Hastings

Andrew Poland

Elizabeth Polanski

Justin Pollard

Gabby Ponce

Dan Pope

Poppy

Zach Powers

John Pratt

Primcess Pamcake

In Memory of Princess Sadie
(aka Baby Kitten)

Tan Qian Ning

Queen Esther & Stacey &
Singa

Queen Esther & Susan &
Justin

Ryley Quest Colligan

Oonagh Quigley

Ariba Qureshi

The Rasmussen Family

Sarah Reardon

Recluse52

Joseph Reid

Kelly Reid

Liz Reid

Justin Reimertz

Sofia Reis Moura

Aaron Reynolds

Jane Richardson

Simon Richardson

Erin Rinker

Gabi Risko

Sarah Riutta

Ana Rivas

Amanda Rivera

George Rivera
Julianne Roberts
Laurel Robinson
Renata Rocha
Daniel, Björk & Agata
    Rocha-Neves
Finn Rock
Brandon Rogers
Callie Rogers
Elizabeth Roller
Roscoe and Athena
Lori Rose
Kaia Rosen
Maggie Rossetti
Janet Rutter
Anna Sabey
Lexi Sablan
Vitalii Saienko
Any Salyer
Jasmin Sanchez
Katy Sardeson-Coe
Maira Saul
Darby Sawyer

Melanie Schmidt
Olivia Schmude
Emily Schneider
Grant Schroeder
Tess Schubert
Felipe dos Santos Schwarz
Jenny Schwarz
Kat Screws
Jazzlyn Sembria
Chloe Sepeda
Katherine Shaw
Faren Shear
Tera Sherwin
Ting Ting Shi
Data, Tabby, Amy, Eddie,
    Sophie, & D.va Shilling
Rebecca Shilling
Jenny Shin
Tim Shrimpton
Anna Simmons
Janet Singer
Alex Skorpinski
Katharine Slater

Kaarin Slotte
Colleen Smallfield
Stephanie Smith
Christine Sockey
Anthony Sorco
Cameron Spickert
Rosslyn Spokes
Spracknel
Josh Squirrell
Marc St-Laurent
Mallory Stalbaum
Imogen Staunton
Susannah Stayter
Amy Stevenson
Danielle & Casper Stewart
Hannah Stewart
Beth Stites
Sandy Stith
Mary Stoicoiu
Bryony Street
Molly Street
Sammy Stroud
Nina Stutler

Simon & Masha Stutler

Tiffany Sucharski

Christina Sumey

Laurel Sutton

Stephanie Szabo

Angie Tanner

Megan Taylor

Lizzie Teasdale

Evan Termini

Will & Ali Thompson

Tom Thorne

Andrew Tippin

Lee Tomkins

Stephen Trotman

Alana Truong

Sarah Turner

Tygerlily

Tziva

Kim Uggerholt

Anne-Marijn Valk

Patricia van Ooy

Ethan Varlin

Kendall Vega

Mark Verschoor

Patricia Vicari

Massiel Villarroel

Carolyn & Stimpy Vogt

Gabrielle Volk

Rachel Volk

Voodoo

Angela Walker

Steve Walker

Matt Walters

Stewart Ware

Julia Weidner

Owen Weitzel

Kim Wheeler

Vivian Wiener

Annette Wilkinson

Daniel Wilkinson

Shay Williams

Ashley & Michael Wills

Abby Wilson

Madeline Winters

David Wohlreich

Emily Wolf

Stephanie Wolf

Melody Woodall-Smith

Lindsay Woodward

Nicole Wooleyhand

Kat Wuelfing Lion

Samir Zahran

Selina Zawacki

ZZ Zhou